# SCHIRMER'S LIBRARY
## OF MUSICAL CLASSICS

Vol. 2065

# FRIEDRICH KUHLAU

# Complete Sonatinas

For Piano

Revised and Fingered by Ludwig Klee

ISBN-13: 978-1-4234-2214-3

# G. SCHIRMER, Inc.

DISTRIBUTED BY

7777 W. BLUEMOUND RD. P.O. BOX 13819 MILWAUKEE, WI 53213

# CONTENTS

# FRIEDRICH KUHLAU
## (1786–1832)

Friedrich Kuhlau was a German-born Danish composer who is best known as a composer of piano music. He was born in Uelzen, a small German town located between Hanover and Hamburg, on September 11, 1786. His father was an oboist, and a military bandsman by profession. At age seven, Kuhlau suffered an unfortunate accident, falling on a slippery street during the winter. As a result, he lost the use of his right eye for the remainder of his life. Kuhlau's earliest musical training is unknown, though it is likely his parents provided lessons as a youth. In 1800, after completing general schooling at the age of 14, Kuhlau moved to Hamburg, studying composition and theory with C.F.G. Schwenke, a highly respected local musician who was a former pupil of C.P.E. Bach. In 1806, Kuhlau had his first pieces published, a set of twelve variations and solos for flute, six waltzes for piano, and three songs for voice and piano.

Napoleon's France annexed Hamburg in 1810 and Kuhlau left the city in fear of being conscripted into the French army, in spite of his physical handicap. Kuhlau fled to Copenhagen, Denmark, under the guise of a concert tour. Once there, Kuhlau worked to establish himself as a composer and performer. He was appointed a court chamber musician in 1813, and his first opera, the singspiel *Røverborgen*, premiered in 1814 at the Royal Theatre, to critical and popular renown. His second opera, *Trylleharpen*, premiered in 1817, but met with significantly less acclaim. Kuhlau traveled to Vienna in 1821 and 1825, the latter trip resulting in a meeting with his musical hero, Beethoven. The two composers spent a boisterous evening of music-making and drinking together, with Beethoven composing a canon on Kuhlau's name ("Kühl, nicht lau," WoO 191) to commemorate the occasion. Kuhlau's greatest public success came for his incidental music to *Elverhøj*, a play written to honor the wedding of the King of Denmark's daughter in 1828. A piece Kuhlau composed for the play was later adopted as one of Denmark's two national anthems ("King Christian Stood by the Lofty Mast"). Shortly after the performance, Kuhlau was appointed honorary professor in the royal court.

While never without work, Kuhlau's appointments did not generate a significant income. As a result, he composed numerous pieces for flute to supplement his earnings, flute music being in high demand during his lifetime in Europe. While these pieces are highly idiomatic, Kuhlau was himself not a flutist, instead relying on a colleague in the royal orchestra for assistance in composing for the instrument. He also composed a significant amount of vocal music, including five operas, over 80 songs, a cantata, and several vocal canons. This music was composed with the latest European styles in mind, showing the influence of Cherubini, Weber, and Rossini.

Tragedy struck often for Kuhlau late in life. Both of his parents, with whom he was very close, died in 1830. On February 5, 1831, fire swept through his apartment building in Copenhagen, destroying all of his unpublished music. As a result of the fire, Kuhlau developed a chest illness that would eventually cost him his life. Kuhlau died in Copenhagen on March 12, 1832. He remains a renowned national music figure in Denmark, and his flute and piano music still enjoy popularity today.

THE PIANO SONATINAS

Kuhlau is best known today as a composer of piano music. He began giving regular piano recitals in 1804 while in Hamburg, and wrote a piano concerto in 1810. His recital programs regularly included Beethoven, and Kuhlau's piano concerto and large-scale piano sonatas were often inspired by the German master. Kuhlau enjoyed significant success as a pianist on his tours to Scandanavia, where his recitals were highly acclaimed, particularly in Sweden. There is no clear evidence regarding Kuhlau's piano teaching; his highly accessible *Sonatinas* were written primarily to augment his income. However, these pieces address significant pedagogical issues, scales and arpeggios in particular, that prepare pianists for the demands of Beethoven's piano music and show a deep understanding of the instrument. They remain staples of most intermediate level pianists. The three sonatinas of Op. 20 were first published in 1819, the six sonatinas of Op. 55 were first published in 1823 in Copenhagen. The three sonatinas (also known as Three Easy Sonatas) of Op. 59 were published in Hamburg in 1824, as were the three sonatinas of Op. 60. Kuhlau's last sonatinas, the four pieces of Op. 88, were published in Copenhagen in 1827.

—*Christopher Ruck*

# Sonatina in C Major

Friedrich Kuhlau
Op. 20, No. 1

a) legato.

a) These small slurs indicate that the last bass-note in one measure should be carefully connected with the first bass-note in the next.

6

# Sonatina in G Major

Friedrich Kuhlau
Op. 20, No. 2

13

Adagio e sostenuto

14

Allegro scherzando

a) Strike the appoggiatura simultaneously with the accompaniment.

# Sonatina in F Major

Friedrich Kuhlau
Op. 20, No. 3

Allegro con spirito

Larghetto
*sostenuto*

a) ♪♪♪  b) Strike the appoggiatura, *f.* simultaneously with the notes for the right hand, *d* and *a.*    c)

Allegro Polacca

# Sonatina in C Major

Friedrich Kuhlau
Op. 55, No. 1

*) Remark: These small slurs indicate that the last bass-note in one measure should be carefully connected with the first bass-note in the next.

# Sonatina in G Major

Friedrich Kuhlau
Op. 55, No. 2

*) Remark: These small slurs indicate that the last bass-note in one measure should be carefully connected with the first bass-note in the next.

Cantabile

Allegretto

# Sonatina in C Major

Friedrich Kuhlau
Op. 55, No. 3

Allegro con spirito

*) Remark: These small slurs indicate that the last bass-note in one measure should be carefully connected with the first bass-note in the next.

Allegretto grazioso

# Sonatina in F Major

Friedrich Kuhlau
Op. 55, No. 4

*) Remark: These small slurs indicate that the last bass-note in one measure should be carefully connected with the first bass-note in the next. a) [image of notation] b) like a.

Andante con espressione

Alla Polacca

# Sonatina in D Major

Friedrich Kuhlau
Op. 55, No. 5

Tempo di Marcia

*) Remark: These small slurs indicate that the last bass-note in one measure should be carefully connected with the first bass-note in the next.

Vivace assai

# Sonatina in C Major

Friedrich Kuhlau
Op. 55, No. 6

Allegro maestoso

45

c) like a.) d) like b.)

Menuet

*) Remark: These small slurs indicate that the last bass-note in one measure should be carefully connected with the first bass-note in the next.

**Trio**

Men. D. C. senza replica, e poi la Coda

**Coda**

# Sonatina in A Major

Friedrich Kuhlau
Op. 59, No. 1

Allegro

# Rondo
### Allegro scherzando

# Sonatina in F Major

Friedrich Kuhlau
Op. 59, No. 2

**Rondo**
Allegro

# Sonatina in C Major

Friedrich Kuhlau
Op. 59, No. 3

Allegro con spirito

# Rondo
Allegro vivace

(This page has been left intentionally blank.)

# Sonatina in F Major

Friedrich Kuhlau
Op. 60, No. 1

Allegro

**Tema**
(Rossini)

Var. 4.

# Sonatina in A Major

Friedrich Kuhlau
Op. 60, No. 2

Allegro con spirito

# Sonatina in C Major

Friedrich Kuhlau
Op. 60, No. 3

a)

Allegro vivace

**Tema**
(Rossini)

Var. 1

Var.2

(This page has been left intentionally blank.)

# Sonatina in C Major

Friedrich Kuhlau
Op. 88, No. 1

108

# Sonatina in G Major

Friedrich Kuhlau
Op. 88, No. 2

Andante cantabile

**Rondo**
Vivace

# Sonatina in A minor

Friedrich Kuhlau
Op. 88, No. 3

Allegro con affetto

# Sonatina in F Major

Friedrich Kuhlau
Op. 88, No. 4

Allegro molto